NAMASTE! MEET MY JESUS

True Stories to Inspire Children Everywhere

Written by Bhagyam Moses

Illustrated by Lisa Prabhakar

World rights reserved. This book or any portion thereof may not be copied or reproduced in any form or manner whatever, except as provided by law, without the written permission of the publisher, except by a reviewer who may quote brief passages in a review.

The author assumes full responsibility for the accuracy of all facts and quotations as cited in this book. The opinions expressed in this book are the author's personal views and interpretations, and do not necessarily reflect those of the publisher.

This book is provided with the understanding that the publisher is not engaged in giving spiritual, legal, medical, or other professional advice. If authoritative advice is needed, the reader should seek the counsel of a competent professional.

Copyright © 2023 Bhagyam Moses
Copyright © 2023 TEACH Services, Inc.
ISBN-13: 978-1-4796-1702-9 (Paperback)
ISBN-13: 978-1-4796-1703-6 (ePub)

Library of Congress Control Number: 2023906895

All scripture quotations, unless otherwise indicated, are taken from The Holy Bible, English Standard Version. ESV® Text Edition: 2016. Copyright © 2001 by Crossway Bibles, a publishing ministry of Good News Publishers.
Scripture quotations marked NOG are taken from The Names of God Bible (without notes) © 2011 by Baker Publishing Group.

Bhagyam Moses has authored a beautiful book for children, based on real life encounters in India. Her loving spirit of sharing and caring for children living in poverty reminds us that, as followers of Jesus of Nazareth, we too are called to show love. Children here, too, can pray expecting to be heard by God. We, too, can pray for children working on construction sites and sleeping on the cold ground.

Noelene Johnsson
Children's Ministries Director at North American Division of Seventh-day Adventists,
Editor of *Mission* for the General Conference of Seventh-day Adventists

These stories are living examples of the Word in our everyday lives. It is so inspiring how Mrs. Moses loved and served the hurting by being the hands and feet of Jesus. We are so happy that she wrote this book by tying each account with the scriptures. It is a great lesson on why we do what we do. This book and the FETCH work truly spurs you to pause, take the situation in, and act on it as we are told in James 1:22—"But be doers of the word, and not hearers only." The story of Rakesh is especially touching as he is preaching the gospel across the world. He, and many of the other kids, trust in Jesus despite all the odds standing against them; their zeal is inspirational.

Mercy Sudhakar Panthulu
Founder of MUCH Hope,
Chairperson of the Bridges Community Church Deaconess Board

Namaste! Meet My Jesus illustrates the intent of our Saviour who extended his gospel of love to children. The author exemplifies this ministry of Jesus in her ongoing relationships with underprivileged children. If you have not experienced the rewards that come from hugging an unloved child, or sharing what you have with kids who have nothing, you must read this book.

Gordon Christo
President, Save the Orphans Please (India)
Secretary, Orphan Relief Society
Former Secretary, Southern Asia Division

The author's plain-spoken emotive book reflects twenty years listening to East Indian children's pain, struggles, victories and dreams. With authenticity and realism, she shares 13 true stories of how impoverished children's prayers changed circumstances, transformed anger into compassion, healed ruptured familial bonds, and set the foundation for a richer tomorrow.

While each story stands in its own uniqueness, taken together they brilliantly unveil the gospel as a powerful transformative agent. Thirteen children internalized one basic message: Jesus, the living King of the Universe, cares deeply for me. What a game changer!! I'm an empowered prayer warrior; not a victim. I can overcome adversities; I can make my dreams a reality.

This book's major take away is both simple and profound. When you are feeling overwhelmed by the difficulties of life, be revitalized by remembering the innocent belief of a child who meets Jesus.

Leanor Boulin Johnson, Ph.D.
Professor Emeritus, Family Studies
School of Social Transformation
Arizona State University
Tempe, Arizona

CONTENTS

1. A Little Construction Worker 5
2. Beggar Children Learn About the Love of Jesus 9
3. Girl with the Messy Hair 11
4. Raghu's Birthday Prayer 15
5. A Baby Girl Is Just as Precious 19
6. God Protects the FETCH Campus from Cobras 21
7. A Little Girl's Need for Prayer 23
8. The Amazing Story of Heaven and Rakesh 27
9. Jesus Answers Kusuma's Prayer 29
10. A Thoughtful Prayer by a Little Girl 33
11. God Answers Susma's Prayer in His Time 35
12. Srinivas: A Thankful Child 39
13. A Crippled Boy Learns About Jesus 43

PREFACE

In 2003, I was still working for a major computer company running a worldwide program and had outsourced the development of a tool in India. Frequent visits to India brought me close to where I was born and brought up. On one visit, I was told my mother had given my father's Daniel and Revelation ministerial materials to one of the believers who was walking the streets of Kukatpally preaching. God blessed his work, and many were baptized. We were told the group had grown, and individual homes were not big enough for them to meet on Sabbath. They wanted us to build a church in Kukatpally. We agreed and built a church in memory of the ministry of our parents—Pastor O.B Jonathan and Salome Jonathan. They started the work in Hyderabad along with Pastor Dan Harris and Pastor Tom Ashlock in the 1950s.

When this church was finally built, we took a group from the Beaverton SDA church in Oregon on a mission trip. Our two daughters, Olivia and Stephanie, were on this mission trip as well. This was the beginning of mission trips each year, with both young and old taking the message of Jesus to many communities in India. More than twenty years of this ministry has taught us that educating children helps pull them out of poverty. We have seen how these children help their families and before you know it, the whole village is blessed.

We served these children by establishing a non-profit organization called FETCH.

F—Feed
E—Evangelize
T—Teach
C—Clothe
H—Heal through the power of Jesus

It has been a blessing to work with these children; to love them, hug them, and rejoice in their successes. More importantly, how meeting Jesus has changed their lives. Giving them simple tools—such as praying to Jesus when they have problems and experiencing His love when they feel unloved and mistreated brought much joy to me. Their faith increased my faith in Jesus, and their love for Jesus increased my love for Jesus. I am thankful for the opportunity that God gave us.

In the end, I know that this is what matters:

> For I was hungry and you gave me food, I was thirsty and you gave me drink, I was a stranger and you welcomed me, I was naked and you clothed me, I was sick you visited me.
> Matthew 25:35-36 (*ESV*)

May the stories in this book give you a glimpse of what I experienced. It is my hope that this will inspire you to reach out to children who are in need and share the love of Jesus with them. It changes them, and you may be surprised at how much it changes you as well.

Author's Intent

This book was written for adults to share and read these stories with children. The audible format is also available to hear these stories directly from the author. It is the author's hope these stories will inspire and bless all who read and hear them.

ACKNOWLEDGEMENTS

    I would like to thank God for the opportunity to minister to the undeserved in India. These true stories of children who acknowledged the love of Jesus in their poverty is only a sample of what I experienced while I was present in their lives.

    I would like to thank my family—Franklin, Olivia, Khari, Stephanie, and Marc for their support, encouragement, and offering advice during the creation of this book. I would also like to thank the FETCH family for their continued support of this ministry. I would like to acknowledge the ministry of my parents—Pr. O.B Jonathan and Salome Jonathan for their tireless ministry in Hyderabad, India. Their godly life has been an inspiration to me throughout my life.

    The completion of this book could not have happened without the help of Lisa Maureen Prabhakar for the beautiful way in which she has worked the pictures and illustrations into the book. I thank her from the bottom of my heart.

    I would like to thank each FETCH child for allowing us to love them and be a part of their lives. I am forever grateful to them for their pure hearts and the constant inspiration they gave me.

LOCATION

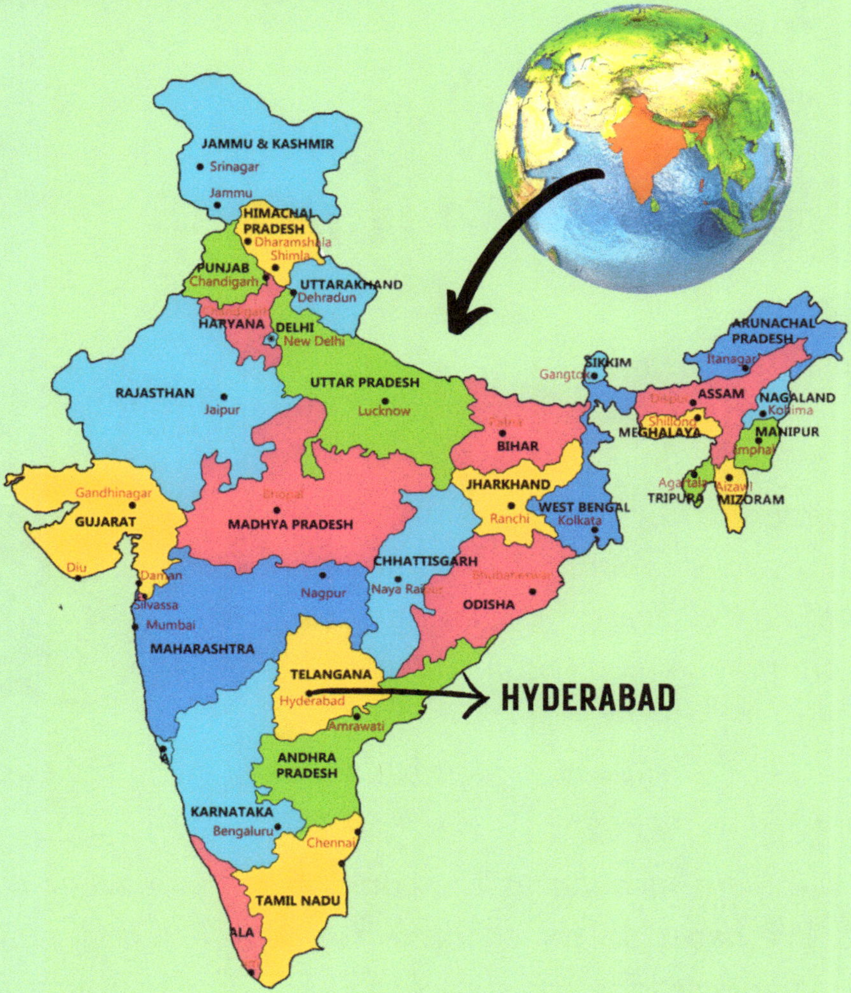

→ HYDERABAD

FETCH School

Meeting Tent

1
A Little Construction Worker

The first FETCH mission trip had its joys and disappointments. God has a way of changing disappointments into blessings. We were hoping that the church we were building in memory of the ministry of my parents in Kukatpally, Hyderabad was still being built and was not completed as planned.

We were meeting at the construction site every day for ten days. We had VBS for children from 4:00 to 6:00 p.m. and an adult evangelistic series from 7:00 to 9:00 p.m. It was exciting to see children coming in to learn songs, listen to Bible stories, do crafts, and coloring beautiful pictures of the stories told that day.

All the children came prepared to attend the meetings. They would wash up and comb their hair, wear clean clothes, and come to the meeting. However, there was a little boy who came wearing dirty, dusty clothes, and his face was not washed, and neither was his hair combed. I felt bad for this little boy and asked him why he did not clean himself before the meeting. He said:

I work all day building this church. I have nowhere to wash myself and these are the only clothes I have.

This broke my heart. I asked him where he slept. He said, "Under the staircase." I looked and it was a bed of sharp stones that were being used for mixing the concrete. My heart began to ache, and I was holding my tears. I told him that I would take care of him the next day and to look for me.

At that time, we were staying in a hotel, but there were stores nearby, and I was able to pick up a mat, sheets, soap, comb, and a towel for him. When we arrived to set up for the meeting, the little boy was there. We were able to get a bucket of water, and the little boy washed himself and cleaned up. He was excited to wear clean clothes.

We were happy to see his beautiful face. What a nice-looking child he was! Who would have thought that under all that dirt and dust there was a handsome little boy waiting to be loved. I asked him where his parents were, and he said he had no parents. I began to wonder how many children were working at construction sites like him. I wanted to help the little children to know about Jesus and His love.

This little boy came every day, and I was able to help him clean up. I fed him so he could enjoy his time at Vacation Bible School. We were disappointed that the church construction was not completed, but God had a different plan. If the construction were completed, we would have never met this little boy. It was through this little boy that the mission began to educate children and connect them with Jesus. God had a plan. Many children like him were educated through the FETCH ministry over the years.

2
Beggar Children Learn About the Love of Jesus

It was a Sabbath day when I was in India. We decided to go to the church that was newly built in the memory of my dad's and mom's ministry in Hyderabad, India. We were seated in Sabbath School when I heard a loud voice at the church gate. I wondered what was going on and went outside. To my surprise, I saw the gatekeeper taking a big stick, chasing away little beggar children.

He was hitting them and telling them that they could not come in. It broke my heart to see little children being treated that way. I immediately tried to stop the gatekeeper.

However, the gatekeeper continued to abuse the children and told me that they were not allowed to come inside the gate. This is when I decided to step in and asked the gatekeeper to step aside and that I will handle the situation. I asked the children to come in and took them to the community center that was recently built. I gave them soap and water to wash themselves and helped them to clean up. I took them inside and tried to find some clothes for them. I found some T-shirts and shorts but no dresses for the girls, but we had beautiful pillowcases. I cut one side of the pillowcase and, with a ribbon, pinned the pillowcases to make beautiful skirts for the girls. The girls looked so cute in their new outfits. I combed their hair and gave them a snack. The divine service was about to start. I took them inside the church and had them sit in front of the pulpit on the carpet. They were so happy to be there. They no longer looked like beggar children. Their faces were glowing with smiles and joy.

I asked the pastor if I could tell a children's story before the sermon. I told them the story of how Jesus asked His disciples not to chase the children away and allow them to come to Him. I was humbled to be able to introduce the loving face of Jesus to these children who had never tasted love. Being chased and beaten was all they knew, but for that moment, they were able to bask in His love.

Jesus said "Let the little children come to me."
Matthew 19:14

After church, I gave them each a care package to take home. The package had some rice and lentils along with a personal hygiene kit that had a comb, toothbrush, toothpaste, bathing soap, washing soap, and a towel. I topped these with a snack and a stuffed animal. You should have seen how thankful they were. I said goodbye to them with the hope that someday they will indeed find Jesus and be in heaven with Him to be loved forever.

3
Girl with the Messy Hair

It was our first attempt at introducing Jesus to a village called Indresam, Hyderabad. There was nothing there except for some huts. We put up a large tent, with loudspeakers blaring, inviting the villagers to come and attend the meetings. With much preparation, we were ready to launch the evangelistic meetings. The tent started filling up with people.

These meetings attract many children and chairs are limited. The children usually sit on the floor to accommodate as many as possible. During one of the meetings, I was sitting on one of the chairs, and a little girl came and sat near my feet. Her hair was a real mess, so I took out my comb and tried to comb her hair. It took me a while to get all the tangles out of her hair. The beauty in her hair came through as we could see her pretty face.

The little girl seemed happy that I combed her hair. She was listening to the songs and stories that were being told. I gave her the comb and told her to come back the next day for the meeting and to be sure to comb her hair. I told her how pretty she looked when her hair was combed. We were so excited that the first meeting went well and the tent was full. People were listening to the sermons and singing songs along with us.

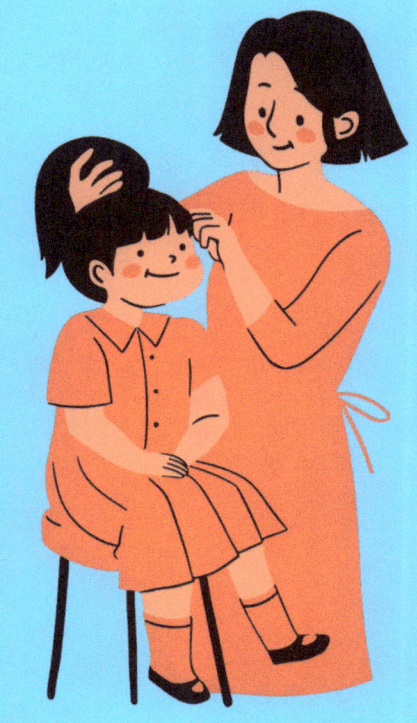

We came back the next day to set up everything for the meeting and to get acquainted with the villagers. As we settled in to start the meeting, the little girl with the messy hair came back to the meeting. She sat down on the floor next to my chair again, just like the first day. So I combed her hair again, wiped her face, and gave her the comb. This happened every night for ten nights. She would come faithfully to the meetings with messy hair and was so happy when her hair was combed and her face cleaned each day. She loved the attention. I asked her what she was doing with all the combs. She said that she was sharing the combs with other children who did not have combs because she knew I would always take care of her. How could you get upset with that?

She loved coming to the meetings. She learned songs and heard beautiful stories about Jesus and His love, but most of all, she learned to pray to Jesus. The meetings finished, and we all went our separate ways. Since we go on these mission trips each year, I would see her now and then. She was a sweet little girl and very hard to forget.

Many years later, we went to visit a government hospital in Sangareddy. We took the patients "care packages" consisting of bathing soap, bar soap for washing clothes, toothbrush, toothpaste, comb, towels, and some fruits. We went to each ward to visit the patients. We gave out these care packages to the patients and sang a song and prayed before we left the ward.

We went to the women's ward, gave out the care packages, sang a song, prayed, and were about to leave the ward when someone came and said that one of the patients wanted to see me. Although she was at the end of the ward and on the last bed, she heard the songs and the prayer. She recognized my voice and wanted to see me.

She was so persistent, that the people insisted that I go to the last bed to see the patient. Although the team was heading to the next ward, I went to the last bed. I was in shock to see the girl with the messy hair in the bed. She was all grown up, but the beautiful face had not changed much. She said, "Madam, do you remember me? You used to comb my hair." I said," Of course, I do. I cannot forget that beautiful face."

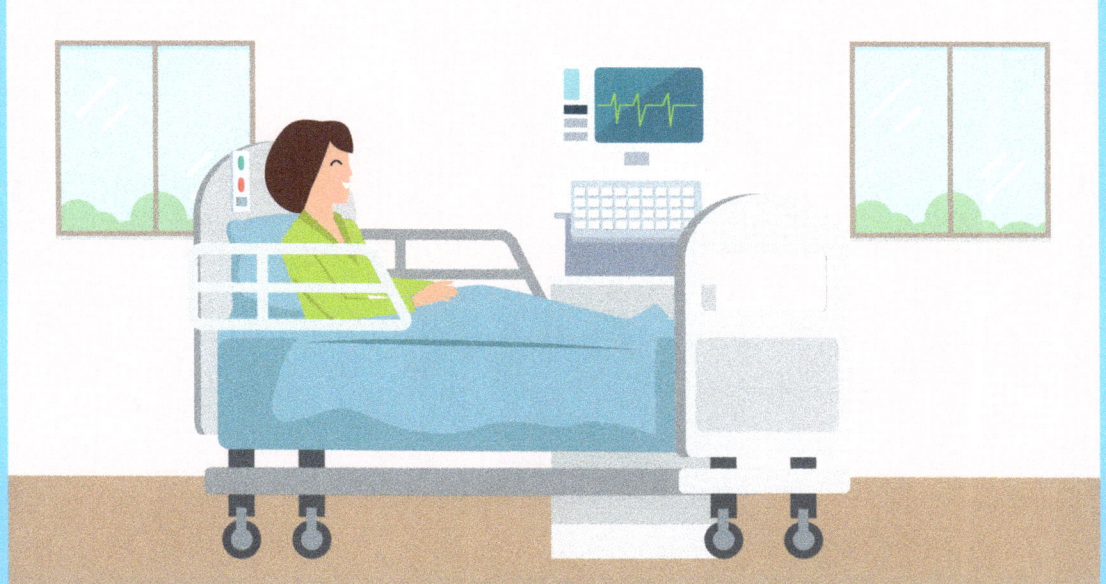

She was burned badly when a gas cylinder exploded in her home. She, along with the whole family, was there being treated for severe burns. I was so sad to hear of the accident. I asked her if she remembered how to pray, and she said, "Yes, madam, I have been praying to Jesus to heal me, my family, and everyone here." I was so happy to hear those words. She had not forgotten Jesus, and her faith in Him brought joy to my heart. You never know how your words and actions will touch someone's heart and bring them to Jesus! I am hoping that I will see that beautiful face in heaven someday when our Jesus comes the second time.

Ask, and it will be given to you.
Matthew 7:7

4 Raghu's Birthday Prayer

Raghu was a little boy that attended the FETCH school in Rameshwarbanda. He studied hard and was always involved with everything that went on at the school. He came to Sabbath School every week regularly and enjoyed singing and listening to Bible stories. Most of all, he was happy to learn that he could talk to Jesus in prayer and that Jesus would answer him.

At the FETCH school, we celebrate the birthdays of people in the United States. People in the US donate money to celebrate their birthdays at the FETCH school. We cook chicken curry and special rice for lunch. We follow that with cake and ice cream in their classroom. The classroom is decorated, and the children wear party hats, and sing happy birthday to the donor as we set up a huge greeting card on the wall of the school. We take a video of the celebration and send it to the birthday person in the US. It is a very beautiful way to celebrate your birthday with 100 loving children who are so happy to taste the life of a rich person in India, even if it is for a day.

Most of the children do not celebrate their birthdays. Some of them do not even know when their birthdays are. Sometimes we have them share the birthdays of the donors. The affluent people in India celebrate their birthdays extravagantly, but Rameshwarbanda is a poor village and they barely have enough food to eat. This makes it so exciting to introduce them to the beautiful birthday celebrations and thanking God for another year of life.

Raghu liked the idea of celebrating birthdays. He wanted to celebrate his little brother's birthday and show his family how a birthday was celebrated. When he went home from school, they had no food to eat that day. This was one of those nights they went to bed hungry. He was feeling so bad. He then remembered about prayer and that if he prayed even for the smallest thing, Jesus would hear his prayer. So he knelt down and prayed Jesus would help him celebrate his brother's birthday.

The next day on his brother's birthday, he prayed again, and when he opened his eyes, there was a knock at the door. A lady brought a tray of goodies for his family.

It is the custom in India to share goodies on festival days. Whether you are a Muslim, Hindu, or a Christian, on their festival day, they share goodies with the neighbors. It was a Muslim festival and the Muslim neighbor brought special treats to Raghu's family who are Hindus.

God works in mysterious ways. Raghu was so excited! He knew it was Jesus our Lord who sent them the goodies. They were able to have a birthday celebration for his brother's birthday that day. Raghu was so happy to share this story of answered prayer in Sabbath School. God is real for these beautiful children, and it fills your heart with joy and happiness to know that we serve a loving and living God who answers prayers—big or small.

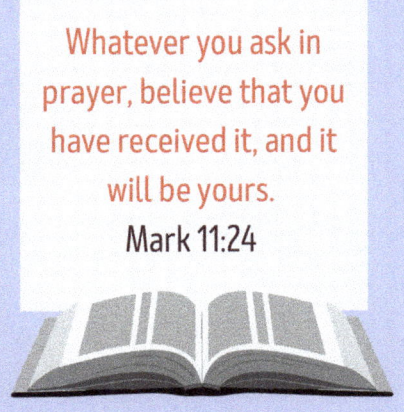

Whatever you ask in prayer, believe that you have received it, and it will be yours.
Mark 11:24

5
A Baby Girl Is Just as Precious

During our mission trips, we visit government-run hospitals. This is where most of the poor go because they receive free care. We take fruits and hygiene kits for the patients. Sometimes we have opp-ortunities to pray with patients and sing for them.

One of the highlights of our hospital visits is to see the newborn babies. We prepare special packages of blankets, hats, booties, and onesies to give out. However, we are often saddened to see how the mothers of baby girls are treated compared to the mothers of baby boys. There is a great celebration and the whole family is there to welcome the baby boy. Unfortunately, girls are viewed as an expense that will put the family in debt for life. In order to get girls married, the family will need to pay a dowry to the groom's family. A dowry is a large amount of money that must be paid to the groom's family to get the girl married. Without this payment, the girl will not be married, and society looks down on families with unmarried girls. Although the dowry system was abolished many years ago, it is still in practice. This situation in the hospital provides us an opportunity to talk to the mothers who are heartbroken and afraid to go home. When a mother hears their daughter is a gift from God and that she is precious, they listen. They have not heard this before. This message is completely different from what they have been hearing. I love to share that both my daughters are doctors, and educating them allowed them to go far in their careers and help many people.

> A gracious woman gets honor.
> Proverbs 11:16

Each mother is surprised and happy to hear about my girls because if my daughters can do it, so can theirs. At this time, telling them about the role they play as mothers in their baby girl's life is critical. Equipping them with the strength and courage that God will provide for them through prayer is the exciting part.

Teaching them a simple prayer that God will hear brings a smile to their faces. Many mothers have been encouraged and connected to God over the years. May His name be glorified! May God give these mothers strength to carry on, despite their circumstances.

6
God Protects the FETCH Campus From Cobras

Our FETCH campus is in a remote village in India called Rameshwarbanda. It is in the outskirts of the city of Hyderabad. We have a day school with 100 students receiving a free education and, most of all, learning about the love of Jesus.

One day, the children told us they saw a huge cobra in the village which is next to our campus. The cobra is a very poisonous snake. I was worried that the snakes would make their way onto our campus. I wanted to make sure that we had the first aid kit to treat the snake bites before they were taken to the hospital. I knew that the children could die without this.

While I was researching on the first aid kit for snake bites, we decided to clean up the campus so that the snakes would not find it appealing to come onto the campus. The gardener was wondering what was happening to the campus and came to talk to me. I started telling him about the snakes and my plans to keep the snakes away and to have a first aid kit should the children be bitten by a snake. He looked at me and was a bit puzzled. He said, "Madam, as long as Jesus is here on this campus, no snakes will enter it. Don't you know that? You tell the children about how God will protect them from all harm and danger."

The gardener was a Hindu. He was attentively listening to the messages, stories, and songs about Jesus that we were teaching the children. I was so ashamed. I did not have the faith of the Hindu gardener. That day, the Hindu gardener preached a beautiful sermon to me—don't get caught up in the logistics of the mission in India while forgetting the almighty power of God that will protect us from all harm.

I am here to witness to you that there have been no reports of snakes on the FETCH campus in India. This is a living testimony of God's protecting care over His people.

My God, my rock, in whom I take refuge.
2 Samuel 22:3

7
A Little Girl's Need For Prayer

It was another busy day at the FETCH campus. Our mission trip program was in full swing with Vacation Bible School, adult evangelistic series, hospital visits, and hut visits. It is full of activities for ten days serving God in various capacities.

It is like you are on a moving train, and you cannot get off until the train stops after ten days. We try to make use of every minute of our time when the mission team is in India. It is a time that is fully occupied and used to serve God. Our motivation is to bring a ray of sunshine to the children in India. There is a tremendous amount of sadness and poverty in the area we serve, and there is much to accomplish in the ten days of the mission trip.

On one of these ten days, I was desperately putting the finishing touches on the sermon that was to be preached that night. The VBS meetings run from 4:00 p.m. to 6:00 p.m. We have a break after that, and then the adult evangelistic meetings start at 7:00 p.m. So I tried to hide from everyone during the break to have the sermon slides ready for the speaker. All of a sudden, I heard a small voice saying, "Madam, madam." I said to myself, "I can't get away from anyone; I just need a few minutes to finish this sermon." I was a bit frustrated. Without looking up, I told the little person that I am busy right now and will come and see her in a few minutes. However, the voice was persistent.

She just needed a few minutes of my time but I just did not have the time. Something inside me made me look up, and I saw a little girl in tears. I thought someone might have said something to hurt her or she did not get a treat. So I asked her, "What is wrong, what is making you cry?" She said while sobbing, "I need you to pray for me and my family." I said, "Of course, I will pray for you and your family. Please tell me what is wrong?" Very reluctantly, she told me that her father was drunk the night before and beat her mother and all her siblings. She was afraid to go home that night because her dad may come back drunk again and beat them.

She asked if I could pray that her father would not do that this again. She insisted by saying, "I know God will answer your prayer."

I was so touched by the little girl's faith, and I was also ashamed of being busy with editing a sermon that I was ready to ignore a real need for prayer. My heart was breaking as I held this beautiful girl, wondering how someone could hurt her. We both prayed with tears streaming from our eyes.

> "Lord, please help this little girl; protect her from her dad. Please change her dad so he will not drink. Take care of this poor family, Lord. Please send your angels to this home so that no harm and danger comes to them. In Jesus' name, amen."

It was hard to let her go home by herself. I wanted to protect her from her environment and take her home, but that was not possible. So I begged God to take care of her and that His power would be made known to her. I knew in my heart that Jesus would protect her better than I could and it was important for this little girl to experience the power of prayer.

We have up to 500 children in attendance for our VBS meetings. I was wondering if I would see this little girl again while I was standing by the gate saying goodbye to the children. As the crowd was leaving, I saw the little girl coming out of the meeting with a smile on her face. I ran to her and gave her a big hug and asked her how things were going at home.

She said, "Jesus heard your prayer. My dad is being nice to us. I keep praying that he will stop drinking. Thank you, madam, for your prayer." My heart was full of joy, and I am so thankful to God.

The village is full of little children who come from families with alcoholic fathers. We have a small window of opportunity to teach the children about prayer and that our loving God will take care of them. What a wonderful God we serve. A God who loves us so much. Telling these children about the home He is preparing for them brings me so much joy. Hope of a better life with Jesus is what these children need to hear. It is a privilege to bring comfort to these children through Jesus Christ.

In everything by prayer and supplication with thanksgiving let your requests be made known to God.
Philippians 4:6

8
The Amazing Story of Heaven and Rakesh

Rakesh is one of the nicest boys in our FETCH school. He is always helpful and takes care of the school campus like it is his own. He is always the best in sports and his studies.

One little boy named Sujay came from the United States with his parents to visit the school. Sujay, being an only child, wanted a brother. On the way to the school, it was decided that God would show him a little boy who would become his brother. Out of the 100 students, Sujay picked Rakesh to be his brother and was convinced that Jesus chose Rakesh. The friendship was immediate. They hung out together the rest of the day.

Sujay and Rakesh kept in touch for many years. Every year we would take a video message from Rakesh to Sujay. On one particular year, Rakesh had the greatest message for Sujay. Here is the message in his own words:

"Hello, Sujay, How are you? When are you coming here to see me again? By the way, I want to tell you something very important. We just finished our VBS meetings. It was great. They told us about heaven and all the beautiful things God is preparing for us. I am excited about heaven. I want to go to heaven. I want you to go with me. Please tell your parents to go with us, and I will tell my parents to go with us. I heard that Jesus will be there and we can talk to Him. This is so exciting. I also heard that there will not be any poverty there. How wonderful is that? Don't forget to tell your parents!
Bye, Sujay."

This message was so pure and convincing. Sujay's parents were touched to hear this message and saw the video many times and were so happy that Rakesh was excited about Heaven. You never know how VBS themes and messages can have an impact on the hundreds of children attending our meetings.

In my Father's house are many rooms.
John 14:2

9 Jesus Answers Kusuma's Prayer

A young girl named Kusuma was a student in our FETCH school. She lived in Rameshwarbanda, which is around twenty miles from Hyderabad, in extreme poverty with her mother, father, and baby sister. Both she and her sister came to school together as their meal at school was the only meal they had each day.

Kusuma was a good student and studied hard. Her favorite part of school was listening to the stories of Jesus and His unconditional love. She learned to pray and sing praises as well.

KUSUMA AND HER SISTER

Kusuma loved hearing about Jesus and how He loved little children. She never experienced love from her father because there was little love expressed in her family. Her home was full of anger and violence. Her father was an alcoholic and abused her mother by constantly beating her and verbally abusing her. Kusuma was not shielded from the violence that alcoholism brought to her home as her father also physically assaulted her and her little sister quite frequently. It was difficult for her to think of anyone being kind or loving to her.

The school faculty and staff were unaware of this abuse because she came to school everyday with a smile. She learned to put on a happy face no matter what happened at home. Her love for Jesus was growing in her heart.

On the last Sabbath before we returned to the United States, we held a routine Sabbath School for all the students. One of the activities was asking the children if they had anything special to share with the group. We saw little Kusuma stand up bravely and share her story. This is Kusuma's story in her own words:

> "The other night, my father came home really drunk. We are used to it, but it was different that night. He had an axe in his hand and was going to chop off my mother's head. I knew this would be possible because several such things happen in our village. Suddenly I remembered what you told us about praying to Jesus for help and that He will help us. I held my sister and closed my eyes, and prayed to Jesus to save my mother. When I opened my eyes, I saw my father drop the axe and run away from the house. I knew it was Jesus who made my father do that. Jesus heard my prayer. I will always trust Him, and I know He loves me. Thank you for teaching us about Jesus."

Kusuma continues to be sponsored by FETCH and she is currently studying in an SDA boarding school. Her sister joined her and they are doing well. Kusuma's mother could not be happier that her daughters will be safe in a boarding school and learning about the love of Jesus.

FETCH provides a Christian education for Kusuma and many other children in need. This opportunity not only allows them to have a great education, but they also learn about the everlasting love of Jesus Christ in a safe environment. FETCH sponsorship not only changes the life of each child but also paves the way to a better life in Jesus. Our hope is that Kusuma and her sister become shining lights for Jesus.

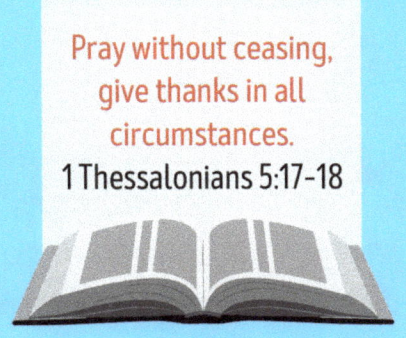

10
A Thoughtful Prayer by a Little Girl

It was Vacation Bible School time again. As soon as the children arrive at the gate of the FETCH school campus, we take them in, ten at a time. We take a few minutes to go over all the rules to make sure they listen to the adults. They are then taken to a place where they get to wash their hands and feet. They come through dusty dirt roads, and they love to wash up. Then they are welcomed into a big tent where the VBS meetings are held.

We start with song service, singing as many as twenty or thirty choruses. The children love to sing and especially enjoy the action songs. After song service, we spend a good amount of time teaching the children how to pray. We encourage children to volunteer and pray in front of everyone each evening. We enjoy having as many children as possible attend our meetings. Surprisingly, we usually do not have major disciplinary problems. However, one particular evening, there were a few children misbehaving.

They were taking small stones and throwing them at the other children. Some of the children were getting hurt, which, of course, was unacceptable. We could not tell who the children were who were throwing the stones. All we knew was the area from where the stones were coming.

If this continued, we would have to send a group of children home. Innocent children along with the guilty children would be sent home. We really did not want to do this, but we were frustrated. Satan is always there to create trouble when everything is going well. While this was going on, a little girl volunteered to pray. She thanked Jesus for everything—for the school, for the VBS meeting, the teachers, parents, etc. She then went on to say:

> "Jesus, there are a few children that are misbehaving; please forgive them. Help them to be good. Please be with the teachers so that they will not get angry and send us away. We want to be at the meeting and learn more about You, Jesus. Amen."

I was shocked at the wisdom of this little girl to pray for these naughty children. She wanted Jesus to forgive them. It was a sermon for me. The attitude of the teachers changed completely. All of a sudden, we had no trouble. The children, after hearing that beautiful prayer, straightened up. The little girl's humble prayer had a huge impact on me and everyone present there. Praise God for this little girl and her faith! Her earnest prayer was answered. We must remember to pray in our difficult times. Prayer is the key that unlocks the storehouse of blessings.

Truly God has listened; He has attended to the voice of my prayer.
Psalm 66:19

11
God Answers Susma's Prayer in His Time

When we opened the FETCH school in Rameshwarbanda, many children who had never gone to school joined our school. We started everyone at the same level and started working with each student individually.

There was one girl, Susma, who was having a hard time remembering things. She would try so hard to remember what she learned but could not recall anything. She was so frustrated. I remember seeing her hitting her head almost in tears. She saw others doing so well, and she felt so bad because she could not perform like them. I felt so bad for her. I tried every method I knew to help her retain what we were teaching her, but it did not work. She was ready to give up. All of a sudden, I realized I did not try the most important thing, which is to pray and ask Jesus to help us.

So, after school, I told her about Jesus and about how He hears our prayers. I promised her that Jesus will hear our prayer if we completely believe in Him. He will answer our prayer and that she will be able to remember what she is taught. She was excited. She agreed that we pray. So we prayed earnestly for

Susma and for Jesus to help her remember what she was taught. She needed memory power to do well in school. I taught her how to pray. We prayed every day, believing that she would do well in school.

She started doing better each day. After a few weeks when I went to the school and stood at the door of the classroom, I saw her standing at the blackboard teaching everyone phonics. She was so good. It brought tears to my eyes. Our God is so powerful, and He answered our desperate prayer. Susma learned to trust in God to do well in school—and her faith was rewarded.

Life was good at the school. One day Susma came to me and asked if Jesus would hear her prayer to bring back her dad, who abandoned them a few years ago. Not knowing her situation and why he left, I was having a hard time answering her question. I said, "God knows best; He will answer your prayer. If He thinks it will be good for you, He will bring your dad back." Years passed by, her question about Jesus answering her prayer and my answer always haunted me. I was hoping that if it was God's will He would send her father back.

Seven years passed by, and we were at the FETCH school when Susma's mother came to the school to talk to me. She wanted to know if we could send Susma to our Seventh-day Adventist boarding school in Nuzvid. To get to Nuzvid, it is an overnight journey by bus or train. I said, "Let us pray about it. If God wants her to go, He will send her." She then mentioned that her father came back and that he was waiting on the road. I went to the gate and asked him to come onto the campus.

When he came in, I told him about how his daughter prayed for him to come back seven years ago. God answered her prayer seven years later. He said he was sorry for what he did. He was young and made a lot of mistakes, but now he is a changed man. He was back to stay and take care of his family. He said he would work hard and support his children's education. He thanked us for what we had done for his family. God knows what is best for us. In His time He will answer our prayers just as He answered Susma's prayer.

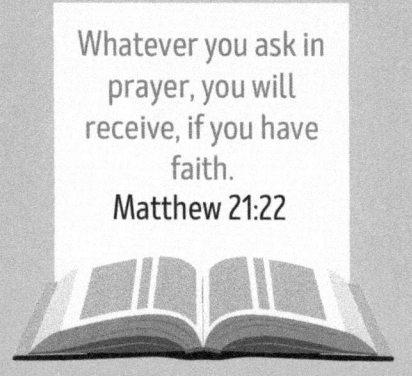

12
Srinivas: A Thankful Child

Srinivas was a little boy who was picked up by FETCH on the streets of Kukatpally, India. Kukatpally is a small town in the suburbs of Hyderabad. Today it is a sprawling metropolis of new Hyderabad. Srinivas used to hang out with his mother and father who sold peanuts on the streets of Kukatpally.

When FETCH approached his parents about sending their children to school, they were excited that their son would have an opportunity to have an education. The nearest Seventh-day Adventist boarding school was in Nuzvid. It was an overnight journey by bus or train to Nuzvid from Kukatpally. Srinivas made the long journey to Nuzvid, leaving home for the first time.

FETCH sent many other children to Nuzvid to study along with Srinivas. The children were excited to be in Nuzvid where they could have three meals a day, sleep in the dorm, wear uniforms and have books to study from. Most of all they were happy to be introduced to Jesus and His love. They learned to sing songs to Jesus, listen to Bible stories, and to pray to a God that would hear their prayers. Every year, the FETCH team of missionaries go to India to provide medical help and to preach the gospel to the disadvantaged of India. This particular year, the team decided to go to Nuzvid and visit the children from Kukatpally to see how they were doing. They rented a bus and made their overnight journey to Nuzvid. The school was excited to see the missionaries from America. The missionaries were also happy to see the children from Kukatpally doing so well in school. They looked healthy and happy.

The missionaries had the opportunity to attend the awards ceremony and their year-end festivities. It was rewarding to see the Kukatpally children getting the gold, silver, and bronze medals for being the first, second, and third ranks in their classes. It was unbelievable to see these children doing so well scholastically. Providing an education to children was, and continues to be, the right thing to do.

Mr. Franklin Moses, the leader of FETCH, was so touched by the children of Kukatpally he got them together and told them how proud he was of their school performance. He gave them Rs.100 (less than $2) to go and buy some treats for themselves. The children were very happy and ran to the store, except for one student.

This was Srinivas. He came to Mr. Moses and told him that he could not take the money and to give it to his father when he returns to Kukatpally. Mr. Moses could not believe what was happening. So he told Srinivas that he would give another Rs.100 to his father and to go along with the other children and buy something for himself. But Srinivas had this to say,

"Sir, you don't understand. My father and mother don't have food to eat and you want me to go and buy sweets to eat. I get three meals a day while they are starving. I think of them every day and feel guilty eating three meals a day and sleeping under a roof, while they have no food or shelter."

When Mr. Moses came back to Kukatpally, he told me this story, which brought tears to my eyes. I wanted to go and see the parents of Srinivas to tell them about the great son they had. So I went to Kukatpally church the following Sabbath. Srinivas' parents started attending this church after their children went to Nuzvid. They would bring their tithe faithfully even though income from selling peanuts on the roadside was meager. After church, I met his parents and was telling them of their thoughtful son and how he refused to take the money because he wanted them to have it. The parents had tears of joy to hear about their son and his love for them, which brought tears to my eyes.

While this was happening, Srinivas joined them because he was back home for the summer holidays. Srinivas reached out and wiped my tears. It was a defining moment for me. I found a mission with a passion to educate children in India and pull them out of their poverty and above all, to introduce them to Jesus and His soon coming. FETCH has been educating children for many years. Through the sponsorship, hundreds of children have discovered Jesus and believe in Him through this program.

Give thanks to the Lord, for He is good.
1 Chronicles 16:34

13
A Crippled Boy Learns About Jesus

Vacation Bible School meetings were a highlight of each FETCH mission trip. The meetings attracted many children.

There was an older boy attending the VBS meetings along with the younger children. He was happy to be there and enjoyed singing and listening to stories about Jesus and His healing power. Unfortunately, his legs did not function. He used his hands like his feet to go from place to place. When the children ran home, he would run just as fast on his hands. Unfortunately, the roads were not paved roads, but dirt roads. There were stones, thorns, sharp objects, and unhealthy garbage everywhere. He also needed to drag his body, and he would get dirty.

We were able to get him crutches. It was hard for him to use them, but he tried. We bought him slippers to protect his hands along with some clothes. After he washed up and wore his new clothes, he looked like a different person. He was so happy to see himself in the mirror. He took both his hands and put them together and said a big thank you. It was a precious moment! What a joy it will be to see him in heaven standing up and walking with Jesus.

> Jesus said to him, "Get up, take up your bed, and walk."
> John 5:8

www.ingramcontent.com/pod-product-compliance
Lightning Source LLC
Chambersburg PA
CBHW041139170426
43199CB00023B/2926